THIS BOOK BELONGS TO

D0409588

A Little Book of

WIT

JARROLD
PUBLISHING

MAE WEST IN A SCENE FROM "EVERY DAY IS A HOLIDAY",
1937

To be natural is such
a very difficult pose to keep up.

OSCAR WILDE

THE TROUBLE with telling a good story
is that it invariably reminds the other fellow of a bad one.

SID CAESAR

It's not the men in my life,
it's the life in my men.

MAE WEST

MY FILMS won't send people out into the streets with axes or anything. The Shirley Temple movies are more likely to do that. After listening to 'The Good Ship Lollipop', you just gotta go out and beat up somebody. Stands to reason.

LEE MARVIN

My main problem is reconciling
my gross habits with my net income.

ERROL FLYNN

A healthy male adult bore consumes
each year one-and-a-half times his own weight
in other people's patience.

JOHN UPDIKE

CHAIRING THE MEETING

William Hogarth 1697–1764

PORTRAIT OF OSCAR WILDE
Henri de Toulouse-Lautrec 1864–1901

An ambassador is an honest man sent to lie abroad for the good of his country.

HENRY WOTTON

HAPPINESS is good health
and a bad memory.

INGRID BERGMAN

One can survive everything
nowadays, except death.

OSCAR WILDE

*N*ext to being witty yourself,
the best thing is to quote another's wit.

CHRISTIAN N. BOVEE

WHOEVER named it
necking was a poor
judge of anatomy.

GROUCHO MARX

A collision is what happens
when two motorists go after the
same pedestrian.

ROBERT BENCHLEY

NEW CAR

Alfred William Strutt 1856–1924

TIME IS a great teacher,
but unfortunately it kills all its pupils.

HECTOR BERLIOZ

A cynic is a man who,
when he smells flowers,
looks around for a coffin.

H. L. MENCKEN

My advice if you insist on slimming –
eat as much as you like, just don't swallow it.

HARRY SECOMBE

THE TOAST
Peter Baumgartner 1834–1911

It's not that I'm afraid to die.
I just don't want to be there when it happens.

WOODY ALLEN

A camel is
a horse designed
by a committee.

ANON

A GOOD STORYTELLER is a person
who has a good memory
and hopes other people haven't.

IRVIN S. COBB

AN INTERESTING STORY
Theodore Lane 1800–1828

GEORGE BURNS, WITH TRADEMARK CIGAR
1982

Life was a funny thing that occurred
on the way to the grave.

QUENTIN CRISP

Too bad all the people who know
how to run the country are busy
driving cabs and cutting hair.

GEORGE BURNS

THERE IS ONLY ONE cure for grey hair.
It was invented by a Frenchman.
It is called the guillotine.

P. G. WODEHOUSE

A STEADY HAND
Edgar Bundy 1862–1922

IN SPITE of the
cost of living,
it's still popular.

LAURENCE J.
PETER

*N*ever go to bed mad,
stay up and fight.

PHYLLIS DILLER

I find that red wine
improves with age.
The older I get
the more I like it.

RAYMOND GEORGE

It usually takes me more than three weeks
to prepare a good impromptu speech.

MARK TWAIN

His mother should
have thrown him away
and kept the stork.

MAE WEST

A woman will sometimes forgive the man who
tries to seduce her, but never the man who
misses an opportunity when offered.

CHARLES MAURICE DE TALLEYRAND

*B*read that must be sliced with an axe
is bread that is too nourishing.

FRAN LEBOWITZ

THE DIFFERENCE between a man and a boy
is that a man's toys cost a lot more.

JANE ACHILLES

A man in love is incomplete
until he has married.
Then he's finished.

ZSA ZSA GABOR

EMBARKATION FOR CYTHERA
Antoine Watteau 1684–1721

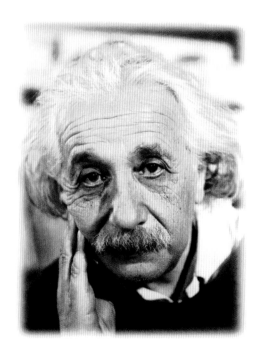

ALBERT EINSTEIN, *German theoretical physicist*, (1879–1955)

The difference between genius and stupidity
is that genius has its limits.

ALBERT EINSTEIN

Better to have loved and lost
a short person than never to have loved a tall.

DAVID CHAMBLE

IF YOU resolve to give up smoking,
drinking and loving, you don't actually
live longer; it just seems longer.

CLEMENT FREUD

I never need to lie,
just re-arrange the truth in my favour.

RAYMOND GEORGE

NEVER lend your car
to anyone to whom
you have given birth.

ERME BOMBECK

Why do people say
'You will never guess what happened to me',
and then expect you to do so?

W. MORRIS

CAUGHT AGAIN
Eugene de Blaas 1843–1931

BEGGING FOR A FAVOUR
Edward Holmes d. 1893

*T*he most popular
labour-saving device
is still money.

PHYLLIS GEORGE

Dogs are sons
of bitches.

W. C. FIELDS

NEVER raise a
hand to your kids.
It leaves your
groin unprotected.

RED BUTTONS

The only person to call a spade a spade
is a gardener.

GRAHAM KEITH

Some couples go over their budgets very carefully
every month, others just go over them.

SALLY POPLIN

AN ADULT Western is where the hero
still kisses his horse at the end,
only now he worries about it.

MILTON BERLE

THE BANKER AND HIS WIFE

Quinten Metsys 1466–1530

When you say you agree to a thing on principle,
you mean that you have not the slightest intention
of carrying it out in practice.

OTTO VON BISMARCK

To get back one's youth
one has merely to repeat one's follies.

OSCAR WILDE

TALK LOW, talk slow,
and don't say too much.

JOHN WAYNE

THE RAKE'S PROGRESS
William Hogarth 1697–1764

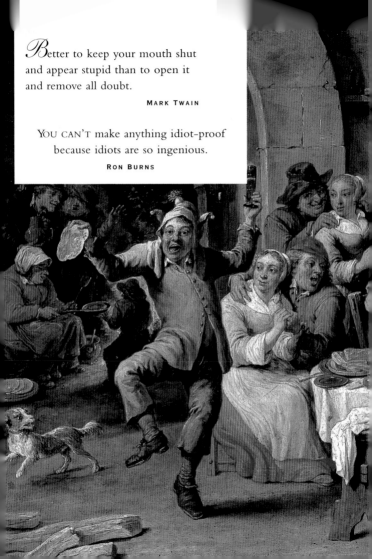

*B*etter to keep your mouth shut and appear stupid than to open it and remove all doubt.

MARK TWAIN

You can't make anything idiot-proof because idiots are so ingenious.

RON BURNS

BAR INTERIOR
Belgian School 19th century

I have a simple philosophy.
Fill what's empty. Empty what's full.
And scratch where it itches.

ALICE ROOSEVELT LONGWORTH

INEXPERIENCE is what makes a young man
do what an older man says is impossible.

HERBERT V. PROCHNOW

I can resist everything except temptation.

OSCAR WILDE

IF I HAD my life to live over again,
I'd live over a saloon.

W. C. FIELDS

I'M NOT a vegetarian
because I love animals;
I'm a vegetarian because I hate plants.

A. WHITNEY BROWN

I hate the thought of resting on my laurels.
Laurels can come to feel very much like holly.

PETER USTINOV

I'm an instant star.
Just add water and stir.

DAVID BOWIE

THE PICNIC IN THE COUNTRY
School of Pietro Longhi 1790

Grandchildren don't make a man feel old;
it's the knowledge that he's married to a grandmother.

ANON

The big print giveth
and the fine print taketh away.

MONSIGNOR J. FULTON SHEEN

EXPERIENCE is the name
so many people give to their mistakes.

OSCAR WILDE

OSCAR WILDE, *Irish wit,*
dramatist and poet (1854–1900)

*I*dealism increases in direct proportion
to one's distance from the problem.
JOHN GALSWORTHY

I NEVER vote for anyone. I always vote against.
W. C. FIELDS

Suburbia is where the
developer bulldozes out
the trees, then names
the streets after them.
BILL VAUGHAN

W. C. FIELDS, *American comedian,*
(1879–1946)

Also in this series
Little Book of Humorous Quotations
Little Book of Naughty Quotations
Little Book of Wisdom

Also available
William Shakespeare Quotations
Winston Churchill Quotations

First published in Great Britain in 1997 by
Jarrold Publishing Ltd
Whitefriars, Norwich NR3 1TR

Developed and produced by
The Bridgewater Book Company

Researched and edited by David Notley
Picture research by Vanessa Fletcher
Printed and bound in Belgium 1/97

Copyright © 1997 Jarrold Publishing Ltd

ISBN 0-7117-0984-X

Acknowledgements

Jarrold Publishing Ltd would like to thank all those who kindly gave permission to
reproduce the words and visual material in this book; copyright holders have been
identified where possible and we apologise for any inadvertent omissions.

We would particularly like to thank the following for the use of pictures:
Bridgeman Art Library, Corbis-Bettmann, e. t. archive, Fine Art Photographic,
Illustrated London News, Mary Evans Picture Library.

Front Cover: *Crispin and Scapin*, Honore Daumier 1808–1879 (e.t. archive)
Frontispiece: *His Favorite Tale*, George Henry 1833–1905 (Bridgeman Art Library)
Back Cover: *Embarkation for Cythera*, Antoine Watteau 1684–1721 (e.t. archive)